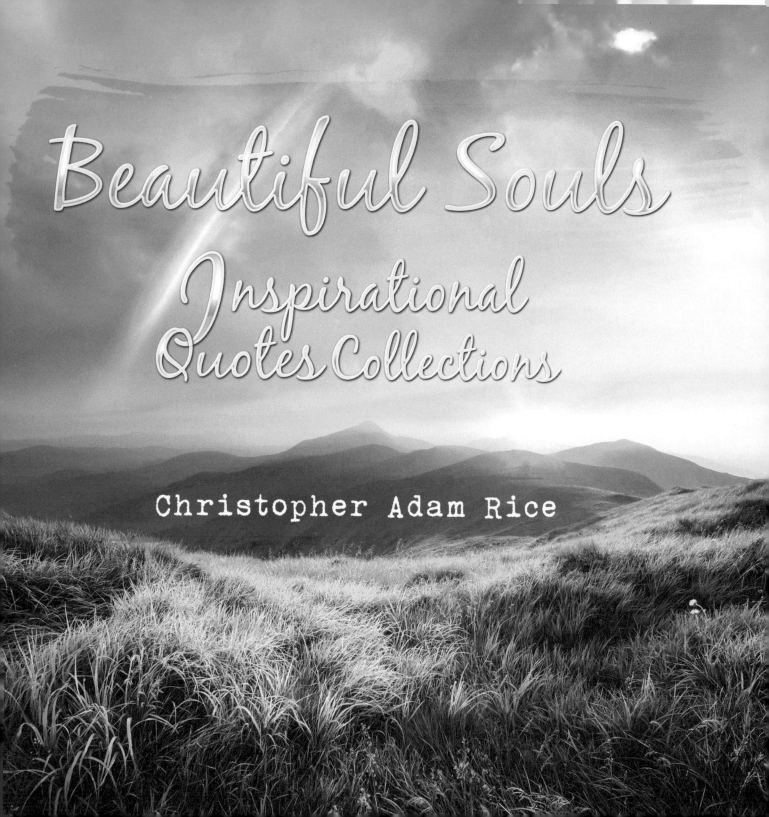

AuthorHouse™
1663 Liberty Drive
Bloomington, IN 47403
www.authorhouse.com
Phone: 1 (800) 839-8640

Published by AuthorHouse 08/15/2020

ISBN: 978-1-5462-4375-5 (sc)
ISBN: 978-1-5462-4374-8 (e)

Library of Congress Control Number: 2018906324

Print information available on the last page.

This book is printed on acid-free paper.

authorHOUSE®

Beautiful souls is a way of thinking that directs our focus on beauty and inspiration. This way of thinking stems from Many years study, of the law of attraction. A simple way of describing the law of attraction is what you focus most upon, you will gravitate towards. So the purpose for the beautiful souls group and book are to Direct our Focus on beauty and inspiration with intentions of gravitating towards it. If we can choose what we gravitate towards in this life, I want Beauty and inspiration. Join us in this way of thinking and be a part of something beautiful.

-Photo by Christopher Adam Rice

What joy I am finding in just
being myself!

- *Christopher Adam Rice*

Christopher Adam Rice

—Photo by Anne Baatz

"Perfection is not attainable, but if we chase perfection we can catch excellence"

- Vince Lomardi

−Photo by Edit Nagy

The human spirit's unquenchable drive for originality and compulsion for creating art is the compelling force of our humanity.

-Unknown

-Photo by Christopher Adam Rice

"The finest steel has to go through the hottest fire"

-Richard M Nixon

-Photo by John Carter

"The more grateful I am, the
more beauty I see"

-Mary Davis

Christopher Adam Rice

−Photo by Mary Andrews

"Family is not an important thing. It's everything."

-Michael J. Fox

-Photo by Sandy Ramsey

"Miracles happen everyday,
change your perception of what
a miracle is and you'll see them
all around you."

-Jon Bon Jovi

-Photo by Jason Rice

Any man who reads too much and uses his own brain too little falls into lazy habits of thinking.

-Albert Einstein

—Photo by Kimi Norton

Love yourself first and everything else falls into line. You really have to Love yourself to get anything done in this world.

-Lucille Ball

—Photo by Bobby Verbaan

Count your blessings, not
your problems.

-Bobby Verbaan

−Photo by Joanne Johnson

The world is a great mirror, it reflects back to you what you are. If you are loving, if you are friendly, if you are helpful, the world will prove loving and friendly and helpful to you. The world is what you are.

-Thomas Dreier

-Photo by Christopher Adam Rice

God lends a helping hand
to the man who tries hard.

-Aeschylus

-Photo by John Carter

"What after all is the object of education? To train the body in health vigor and grace so that it may express the emotions in beauty and mind with accuracy and strength."

-Annie Besant

13

−Photo by Bobby Verbaan

"Every day I am thankful in knowing my strengths are bigger than my fears."

-Bobby Verbaan

-Photo by Babette Van Abs

"Your library is your paradise."

-Desider vs Erasmus

Christopher Adam Rice

−Photo by Hanna Garcia

"A little piece of heaven."

-Hanna Garcia

-Photo by Christopher Adam Rice

"If I ruled the world. I would look this relax too."

-*Christopher Adam Rice*

Christopher Adam Rice

-Photo by Dellene Garlock

You have within you, something magical. It can't be seen. It can only be felt from within. But it exists as surely as you exist. It is your spirit—your human spirit.

-Toni Sorenson

-Photo by Kelly Dinning

"The key is not to prioritize what's on your schedule but to schedule your priorities"

-*Stephen R. Covey*

Christopher Adam Rice

−Photo by Hannah Garcia

"It is spring again. The earth
is like a child that knows
poems by heart."

-Rainer Maria Rilke

−Photo by Pamela Yvonne Mangus

"She is water powerful enough to drown you, soft enough to cleanse you, deep enough to save you."

-Adrian Michael

Christopher Adam Rice

-Photo by Bella Bernier

"You owe it to yourself to reach for your inner self."

-Bella Bernier

–Photo by Christopher Adam Rice

"Not all things are easy, but holding a good attitude
will lighten the weight of any task."

-Christopher Adam Rice

Christopher Adam Rice

−Photo by Debbie Wherrett

"There is only one happiness in this life. To love and be loved."

-George Sand

-Photo by Kim Lamberti Wennberg

"Strength does not come from winning. Your struggles develop your strength. When you go hardships and decide not to surrender, that is strength."

-Arnold Schwarzenegger

Christopher Adam Rice

-Photo by Amy Brandenburg

"The human spirit holds strength beyond measure. The kind that will break down walls of all the blocks that come our way."

-Nikki Rowe

−Photo by Pamela Yvonne Mangus

"Love is a chain of love as
nature is a chain of life."

-Truman Capote

Christopher Adam Rice

-Photo by Kenny Crewse

There's no magic
more powerful than
the human spirit.

-Vic James

-Photo by Katie Arrington

"Happiness is like a butterfly which when pursued is always beyond our grasp, but if you will sit down quietly, may alight upon you."

-Nathaniel Hawthorne

Christopher Adam Rice

−Photo by Declan O'Donoghue

To the world you may be one person, but to one person, you may be the world.

-*Bill Wilson*

-Photo by Christopher Adam Rice

Only together we will grow, we are all beautiful parts that make up the whole.

-Christopher Adam Rice

Christopher Adam Rice

-Photo by Christopher Adam Rice

The lips of wisdom are closed except to the ears of understanding.

-Hermes Trismegistus

-Photo by Declan O'Donoghue

Nothing makes me feel more Alive than when I see the magic in my children's eyes.

-Declan O'Donoghue

Christopher Adam Rice

-Photo by Anne Baatz

"Know who creates this beauty brings comfort"

-Anne Baatz

-Photo by Christopher Adam Rice

Oh the hill

Such a tall hill

I take on the fear

Of knowing what comes next

I climb with determination

I climb with curiosity

With that very moment

I take my next breath

And there I see

The most beautiful sight
there can possibly be

Her blazing glow reflection

On the beautiful sea

The wind skimming past my ears

And from that moment on

I let go of all my fears

-Leah Gannon

Christopher Adam Rice

-Photo by Daniel Rice

"Never lose hope, because when the sun goes down, the moon and stars come out."

-Bella Bernier

-Photo by Amy Brandenberg

The heart is an instrument of the soul, when the heart is in tune,
the soul may then play a beautiful symphony.

-*Christopher Adam Rice*

−Photo by Monika Schold

"There are two ways of spreading light: to be the candle or the mirror that reflects it."

-Edith Wharton

−Photo by John Carter

"When the roots are deep,
there is no need to worry
about the wind."

-Unknown

Christopher Adam Rice

-Photo by Christopher Adam Rice

It's no jet plane,

But when I ride,

I'm flying

-Christopher Adam Rice

-Photo by Kelly Dinning

People are like stained-glass windows. They sparkle and shine when the sun is out, but when the darkness sets in, their true beauty is revealed only if there is a light from within.

-Elisabeth Kübler-Ross

-Photo by Christopher Adam Rice

The real meaning of enlightenment is to gaze with undimmed eyes on all darkness.

-Nikos Kazantzakis

The pictures in this book we're taken in our everyday lives. Our perspectives of what we see creates our experience in OUR world. Our power as Beautiful Souls is to reshape our surroundings through a shift in our perspective. A shift towards what we find more beautiful and inspiring.

A portion of all sales is donated to our charity Beautiful Souls Inc. EIN-84-2229459

Alexander James
Director and co-founder of Beautiful Souls Inc.
Weareallbeautifulsouls@gmail.com

Chef executive officer(ceo) & founder of MonsterKong Marketing
Social media & digital marketing agency
www.monsterkongmarketing.com

Christopher Adam Rice
Director and co-founder of
Beautiful Souls Inc. EIN 84-2229459
www.beautifulsouls.co
weareallbeautifulsouls@gmail.com

"We seek Beauty and Inspiration in the World so that we may
find it within Ourselves." Christopher Adam Rice

https://www.facebook.com/groups/410227172755306/

BEAUTIFUL SOULS

Printed in the United States
By Bookmasters